W9-CAF-424

Table of Contents

Chart

Legal Status of Federal-Sector Arbitration

Preliminary Observations: Federal and Private
Sectors Compared

Much of the vast body of substantive and procedural principles developed by private-sector labor-management arbitration in the United States is equally applicable at the federal level and in other public-sector areas as well.[1] While it is true that many activities and fact situations in the public sector differ from those in private industry, the principles being applied in federal and other public-sector arbitration generally are the same time-tested principles that evolved through the years in private-sector arbitration. This is not surprising, even apart from the fact that quite commonly a given arbitrator serves both the public and private sectors. Nor is it surprising, human nature being as it is, that arbitration proceedings are no less adversary in nature in the public sector than in the private sector.[2]

The significant differences or variations that do exist between federal-sector and private-sector arbitration relate principally to certain aspects of legal status. The scope of the duty to bargain; the status of management rights; the degree of required adherence by the arbitrator to laws, rules, and regulations; and the scope of review of the arbitrator's decision are probably the most important areas of difference or variation (Note that differences in these areas also may affect the arbitrability of issues and the scope of the arbitrator's remedy power, in some cases making it narrower in the federal than in the private sector). These matters are treated in the materials that follow, but the reader will quickly observe that the materials also deal with other special features of labor-management dispute settlement in the federal sector.

An understanding of the role of contractual grievance procedures and arbitration in the federal sector is aided by some knowledge of the historical and present setting within which they exist.

---

[1] For those principles, see Elkouri and Elkouri, HOW ARBITRATION WORKS (3rd ed.; The Bureau of National Affairs, Inc., 1973).

[2] Illustrating the extremely adversary nature of some public-sector grievance disputes and their handling, see National Labor Relations Board, 68 LA 279 (Sinicropi, 1977).

1

The scope of the federal-sector materials that follow has been made more expansive with this thought in mind.

The Executive Orders and the Civil Service Reform Act of 1978

In 1962 federal employees were granted organizational and bargaining rights by President Kennedy's Executive Order 10988. These rights were further advanced by President Nixon's Executive Order 11491 of 1969, which made certain changes to coordinate, strengthen, and clarify the program.[3]

Executive Order 10988 permitted the use of advisory (not binding) arbitration; and such arbitration was in fact used for representation, bargaining unit, and grievance issues in federal employment.

Under Executive Order 11491, provision was made for representation disputes, grievances, and contract-negotiation disputes as follows:

- Provision was made for representation elections under the supervision of the Assistant Secretary of Labor for Labor-Management Relations, and this official decided questions concerning the appropriate unit.
- Negotiated procedures could provide for arbitration of employee grievances and of disputes over the interpretation or application of collective agreements between federal agencies and labor organizations. Either party could file exceptions to an arbitrator's award with the Federal Labor Relations Council.
- Arbitration or third-party factfinding could be used to resolve negotiation impasses, but only when authorized by the

---

[3] For informative articles on the federal sector program under E. O. 11491 as amended by subsequent Executive orders, see Gamser, *Back-Seat Driving Behind the Back-Seat Driver: Arbitration in the Federal Sector*, PROCEEDINGS OF THE THIRTY-FIRST ANNUAL MEETING OF NAA (The Bureau of National Affairs, Inc., 1979), p. 268; Porter, *Arbitration in the Federal Government: What Happened to the 'Magna Carta'?* PROCEEDINGS OF THE THIRTIETH ANNUAL MEETING OF NAA (The Bureau of National Affairs, Inc., 1978), p. 90; Frazier, *Labor Arbitration in the Federal Service*, 45 G.W. L. REV. 712 (1977); Tobias, *The Scope of Bargaining in the Federal Sector: Collective Bargaining or Collective Consultation*, 44 G.W. L. REV. 554 (1976); Aronin, *Collective Bargaining in the Federal Service: A Balanced Approach*, 44 G.W. L. REV. 576 (1976); Williams, *Accommodation of Jurisdiction Over Federal Labor Disputes*, 44 G. W. L. REV. 604 (1976); Nesbitt, LABOR RELATIONS IN THE FEDERAL GOVERNMENT SERVICE (Bureau of National Affairs, 1976); Kagel, *Grievance Arbitration in the Federal Service: How Final and Binding?* 51 OREGON L. REV. 134 (1971); Shaw & Clark, *Determination of Appropriate Bargaining Units in the Public Sector: Legal and Practical Problems*, 51 OREGON L. REV. 152 (1971); Wollett, *The Bargaining Process in the Public Sector: What Is Bargainable?* 51 OREGON L. REV. 177 (1971); Weber, *Federal Labor Relations: Problems and Prospects*, ARBITRATION AND THE PUBLIC INTEREST (The Bureau of National Affairs, Inc., 1971) p. 148.

Federal Service Impasses Panel (which itself could make a final decision on the impasse).

Prior to the promulgation of the Executive orders and, indeed, throughout their periods of enforcement the United States Civil Service Commission exercised broad statutory jurisdiction over federal employment. The Commission had functions of executive, rulemaking, and judicial nature. Its judicial function related to the rights of federal employees and the protections accorded them under the merit system. Under the Civil Rights Act of 1964 and several other statutes it also had responsibility for enforcement of the policy against discrimination in federal employment. Thus, for merit-system and discrimination issues the federal employee had remedies before the Civil Service Commission. Such remedies have been called "statutory remedies," as distinguished from the "contractual remedies" of the grievance procedure and arbitration provided under collective bargaining agreements. Under the Executive order program the existence of a statutory remedy for an issue preempted or foreclosed applicability of a contractual remedy for the issue. This was changed, however, by the Civil Service Reform Act of 1978.

Effective January 1979 major changes regarding federal employment were made by Presidential Reorganization Plan No. 2 of 1978 (which automatically became law when neither House of Congress disapproved within the specified time) and the Civil Service Reform Act of 1978. The Civil Service Commission was abolished as such and replaced by two agencies—the Office of Personnel Management and the Merit Systems Protection Board. The mechanics of this change were as follows: (1) the Civil Service Commission was "redesignated the Merit Systems Protection Board" with the "hearing, adjudication, and appeals functions" of the former Civil Service Commission (except with respect to examination ratings); and (2) the Office of Personnel Management was established to perform other functions of the former Civil Service Commission.[4]

The Federal Labor Relations Council established by Executive Order 11491 was replaced by the Federal Labor Relations Authority with statutory status.[5] The Federal Service Impasses Panel established by Executive Order 11491 was continued and given statutory status.[6] Thus, the labor-management relations and dis-

---

[4] 5 U.S.C.A. §§ 1101 et seq. (Reorganization Plan No. 2 is published with the annotations to § 1101).
[5] 5 U.S.C.A. §§ 7104, 7105.
[6] 5 U.S.C.A. § 7119.

pute-settlement program that had existed for federal employment under the Executive Orders has now been codified (with some major changes).[7]

Another significant change was made by Presidential Reorganization Plan No. 1 of 1978 (which also became law automatically when it was not disapproved by either House of Congress within the specified time). This change was that responsibility for enforcement of the policy against discrimination (civil rights, age, equal pay, handicapped individuals) in federal employment was transferred from the Civil Service Commission and certain other agencies or officials to the Equal Employment Opportunity Commission.[8]

The Agencies and Their Role

Office of Personnel Management (OPM). "The Office of Personnel Management is an independent establishment in the executive branch."[9] The OPM succeeded to Civil Service Commission functions relating to recruitment, measurement, ranking, and selection of individuals for initial appointment and competitive promotion in federal employment.[10] As its name suggests, the OPM's functions are essentially executive or managerial in nature. It is the MSPB (Merit Systems Protection Board) rather than the OPM which now exercises adjudication and appeals functions relating to federal employee grievances.

Merit Systems Protection Board (MSPB). By the Civil Service Reform Act of 1978 the Merit Systems Protection Board has jurisdiction over a broad range of grievance claims or issues involving federal agency actions affecting employees, including discrimination claims that are combined or mixed with merit-system claims.[11]

Also of significance is the MSPB's authority to review rules and regulations issued by the OPM, and to declare any rule or regula-

---

[7] However, 5 U.S.C. § 7135 provides that Executive Order 11491 and certain other Executive orders "shall remain in full force and effect until revised or revoked by the President, or unless superseded by specific provisions of [the Civil Service Reform Act] or by regulations or decisions issued pursuant to [the Act]." For summaries of the codified federal-sector program, see Ingrassia, *Reflections on the New Labor Law,* 30 LABOR L. J. 539 (1979); Frazier, *Labor-Management Relations in the Federal Government,* 30 LABOR L. J. 131 (1979).

[8] Reorganization Plan No. 1 is published with the annotations to 42 U.S.C.A. § 2000e-4. On discrimination complaints in federal employment, see Martin, *Equal Employment Opportunity Complaint Procedures and Federal Union-Management Relations: A Field Study,* 34 ARB. J. 34 (1979), where many articles on the subject are collected.

[9] 5 U.S.C. § 1101.

[10] These functions are enumerated in 5 C.F.R. § 300.101.

[11] Regarding the Board's composition, its Special Counsel, and its powers and functions, see 5 U.S.C. §§ 1201-1205, 7701, 7702. For merit system principles and protections that may become involved in employee claims before the MSPB, see 5 U.S.C. §§ 2301, 2302. The MSPB was initially established by Reorganization Plan No. 2 of 1978 to exercise "the hearing, adjudication, and appeals functions" of the Civil Service Commission.

tion invalid if the rule or regulation or its implementation would violate or lead to violation of any prohibited personnel practice adversely affecting employees (Certain personnel practices are prohibited by statute because they are contrary to merit system principles).[12]

Federal Labor Relations Authority (FLRA). The Federal Labor Relations Authority succeeded the Federal Labor Relations Council and performs various important functions in federal labor-management relations.[13] In general, its functions are

1. To "provide leadership in establishing policies and guidance relating to" labor-management relations matters under Title VII of the Civil Service Reform Act of 1978
2. To determine appropriate units and to conduct representation elections for collective bargaining under the Act[14]
3. To prescribe criteria and resolve issues relating to consultation rights under the Act
4. To resolve issues relating to the duty to bargain
5. To prescribe criteria and resolve issues relating to the determination of "compelling need" for agency rules or regulations (The duty to bargain extends to any matter which is the subject of rules or regulations of any agency or national subdivision thereof *only if* the FLRA has determined that "no compelling need" exists for the rule or regulation. This becomes an important consideration in the arbitration of some grievances.)
6. To resolve unfair labor practice complaints
7. To resolve exceptions to arbitration awards.

Equal Employment Opportunity Commission (EEOC). The Civil Rights Act of 1964 established the Equal Employment Opportunity Commission and placed basic responsibility upon it for implementation and enforcement of the Act's prohibitions against discriminatory employment practices.[15] Also, Reorganization Plan No. 1 of 1978 transferred to the EEOC the responsibility for equal opportunity in federal employment which had been vested in the Civil Service Commission pursuant to § 717 of the Civil Rights Act of 1964; it also transferred enforcement functions for age discrimination, equal pay, and federal employment of handicapped indi-

---

[12] See 5 U.S.C. §§ 1205(e) [review authority], 2301 [merit system principles], 2302 [prohibited personnel practices].

[13] See 5 U.S.C. §§ 7104 [appointment of FLRA members and General Counsel], 7105 [FLRA functions].

[14] The NLRB rather than the FLRA handles representation matters for the Postal Service. See 39 U.S.C. §§ 1202-1204.

[15] See 42 U.S.C. §§ 2000e-4, 2000e-5.

viduals to the EEOC from the agency or official previously exercising those responsibilities.

General Accounting Office (GAO). "[I]f considered necessary by the Comptroller General, the General Accounting Office shall conduct audits and reviews to assure compliance with the laws, rules, and regulations governing employment in the executive branch and in the competitive service and to assess the effectiveness and soundness of Federal Personnel management."[16]

Federal Service Impasses Panel (FSIP). By statute the "Federal Service Impasses Panel is an entity within the [Federal Labor Relations] Authority, the function of which is to provide assistance in resolving negotiation impasses between agencies and exclusive representatives."[17] The statute provides that if an impasse is not resolved by the Federal Mediation and Conciliation Service or by other third-party mediation, either party may request the FSIP to consider the matter; or the parties may agree to a procedure for binding arbitration (but only if the procedure is approved by the FSIP). If the parties do not reach a settlement after assistance by the FSIP, it may conduct hearings on the matter and resolve it by action which is binding on the parties during the term of the agreement.

Channels for Processing Federal-Sector Grievances

The channels for processing federal-sector grievances vary, depending upon the subject of the grievance and the grievant's choice of statutory options. Channels and options are shown in skeletal form in the chart on page 8. Relevant statutory sections are cited to indicate the statutory basis and as a source of greater detail. In the latter regard, it is stressed that the chart does not show time periods within which action is to be taken or decision rendered.

When using the chart it is imperative that the explanatory notes (*a* through *i*) be considered carefully. Also, use of the chart will be greatly aided by reading the related topics that follow.

Role and Scope of Federal-Sector Grievance Procedure and Arbitration

The basic function of the grievance procedure and arbitration in private employment is to assure compliance with the collective

---

[16] 5 U.S.C. § 2304, which also specifies that the GAO shall submit an annual report to the President and Congress on MSPB and OPM activities, including an analysis of whether OPM actions conform to merit-system principles and are free from prohibited personnel practices. Also see, below, the section entitled "Comptroller General's Review Role."

[17] 5 U.S.C. § 7119. Different statutory provisions exist for the Postal Service. See 39 U.S.C. § 1207, which specifies use of a "factfinding panel" and arbitration under the auspices of the FMCS.

bargaining agreement. While this is also a key function of the griev-ance procedure and arbitration in the federal sector, there they have dual basic roles. The second and also very important function of the grievance procedure and arbitration in the federal sector is to review or police compliance with controlling laws, rules, and regu-lations by federal agency employers and employees alike.[18]

The dual role of the grievance procedure and arbitration prob-ably was a principal factor in the congressional decision (1) to spe-cify that each collective agreement in the federal sector "shall" pro-vide a grievance procedure with arbitration, (2) to specify that all grievances "shall" be subject to the grievance and arbitration proce-dures except those specifically excluded by the collective agreement or statute, and (3) to define the term "grievance" very broadly.

Arbitral disposition of federal-sector grievances will often be governed or materially affected by laws, rules, and regulations apart from the collective agreement; another highly significant factor is that important areas of unilateral management control in the federal sector exist by statute. For some matters in the federal sector, the collective agreement and custom cannot be made the controlling "law of the plant."

Turning now to the detailed language of the statutes, we note first that it is required by statute that each collective bargaining agreement in the federal sector "shall provide procedures for the settlement of grievances, including questions of arbitrability."[19] The statute also requires that each agreement "shall . . . provide that any grievance not satisfactorily settled under the negotiated grievance procedure shall be subject to binding arbitration which may be invoked by either" the union or the federal agency employer.

The same statute provides, with only two exceptions, that the contractual grievance procedure *and* arbitration (since the griev-ance procedure must provide for arbitration) "shall be the exclusive procedures for resolving grievances which fall within its cover-age."[20] The two exceptions involve certain subjects or issues for

---

[18] Illustrating this role of the grievance procedure and arbitration in the federal sector, see Arbitrator Goodman in 72 LA 57, 61-62; Leventhal in 72 LA 44, 45-47; Tsukiyama in 71 LA 1138, 1142, 1147; Jackson in 71 LA 463, 465; Gottlieb in 70 LA 1291, 1295; Griffin in 70 LA 360, 365; Whitman in 69 LA 1097, 1098; Dunn in 68 LA 211, 213.

[19] 5 U.S.C. § 7121. The Postal Service statute states that the collective agreement "may" provide grievance and arbitration procedures. 39 U.S.C. § 1206(b).

[20] If the union decides not to arbitrate and the issue is one which can only be taken to the contractual grievance and arbitration procedures (see Category I in the chart below), the employee may be left with no remedy unless some "duty of fair representation" issue exists (as-suming the "duty of fair representation" applies in the federal sector as it does in private em-ployment). For some issues (Category I) an employee not in the bargaining unit [contd., p. 10]

Channels for Processing Federal-Sector Grievances*

	Grievance Subject	Processing Channels
Category I	All subjects (issues) except those included below in Categories II, III, and IV or those the parties have excluded from the grievance procedure or which are expressly excluded by 5 U.S.C. § 7121.[a] *Statutes:* 5 U.S.C. §§ 7121, 7122, 7123.	Grievance Procedure → Arbitration → FLRA[b] (FLRA decision is final except that the U.S. Court of Appeals review of the FLRA final orders is available if an unfair labor practice issue is involved.)
Category II	Reduction in grade or removal for unacceptable performance. Removal, suspension for more than 14 days, reduction in grade or pay, furlough of 30 days or less. *Statutes:* 5 U.S.C. §§ 4303, 7121, 7122, 7512, 7701, 7703 (court review standards stated here).	Grievance Procedure → Arbitration[c] → U.S. Court of Claims or U.S. Court of Appeals *Or,* at the employee's option (commencing one channel bars the other) MSPB → U.S. Court of Claims or U.S. Court of Appeals
Category III	Discrimination (race, color, religion, sex, national origin, age, sex/equal pay, handicapped condition, to the extent that any such discrimination is prohibited by federal statute)[d] *Statutes:* 5 U.S.C. §§ 2302, 7121; 42 U.S.C. §§ 2000e-5, 2000e-16[e]; Reorganization Plan No. 1 of 1978.	Grievance Procedure → Arbitration → FLRA → EEOC → U.S. District Court[e] *Or,* at the employee's option (commencing one channel bars the other, but the employee can reach the EEOC by either) Complaint to the employee's Agency → EEOC → U.S. District Court (employee has option to go directly to District Court from employee's Agency)[e]
Category IV	Mixture of a discrimination issue and other issue.[f] *Statutes:* 5 U.S.C. §§ 7121, 7702, 7703(b)(2).	Grievance Procedure → Arbitration → FLRA[g] → MSPB[h] → U.S. District Court[i] *Or,* at the employee's option (by either channel employee can reach the MSPB and can petition the EEOC) Complaint to employee's Agency → MSPB[h] → U.S. District Court[i] (employee also has option to omit appeal to the MSPB and go directly to U.S. District Court[i])

*See explanation of grievance-processing channels, p. 6.

Channels for Processing Federal-Sector Grievances
CHART ABBREVIATIONS

MSPB: Merit Systems Protection Board
FLRA: Federal Labor Relations Authority
EEOC: Equal Employment Opportunity Commission

NOTES

[a]If the issue is excluded from the grievance procedure or if the employee is outside the bargaining unit, then any statutory remedy (such as consideration by the MSPB) would be used.

[b]What FLRA ultimately does in its review may be significantly affected by the role and actions of the Comptroller General. See sections on Comptroller General in text.

[c]For Category II issues the arbitrator is governed by the same criteria and standards that would govern the MSPB. See 5 U.S.C. §§ 7121(e)(2), 7701(c)(1)&(2).

[d]Section 2302 also prohibits marital status or political affiliation discrimination to the extent prohibited by any law, rule, or regulation; the remedy here would be the grievance procedure or the MSPB. See § 7121(d).

[e]The U.S. District Court action specified by these sections is an original action and thus is a less restricted form of judicial proceeding than that indicated above for Category II grievances, for which the statute specifies limited grounds on which the court may disturb results reached below. Also, the U.S. District Court proceedings indicated below for Category IV grievances are similarly less restricted than the judicial review on limited grounds which applies to Category II grievances.

[f]The channels indicated for this category apply where employee's agency takes action appealable to the MSPB and the employee alleges discrimination as a basis for the agency's action. A Category III issue combined with a Category II issue would qualify, as would a Category III issue combined with any other issue appealable to the MSPB—MSPB has jurisdiction over many agency actions affecting employees in addition to those in Category II. However, *if* the contractual grievance procedure covers a matter not involving a Category II subject and/or discrimination, the channel indicated under Category I is the only one available.

[g]If the arbitration award involves one of the subjects included under Category II, it would not be appealable to the FLRA but would go from arbitration directly to the MSPB.

[h]Instead of going directly to court from the MSPB the employee has the option of petitioning the EEOC to consider the MSPB decision. If such request is denied, employee proceeds to U.S. District Court.[i] If the request is granted but the EEOC concurs with the MSPB, the employee then goes to U.S. District Court.[i] If the EEOC disagrees with the MSPB, the matter is returned to the MSPB; and (depending upon whether the MSPB adopts the EEOC decision) from there it goes either directly to U.S. District Court[i] or to a Special Panel and then to U.S. District Court.[i]

[i]In the U.S. District Court in these "mixed" cases the employee has the right to trial de novo. 5 U.S.C. §§ 7702(e)(3), 7703(c). Moreover, if a grievance is taken to the employee's agency and no decision issues within the statutory time limit, the employee may either proceed to the MSPB or commence an original action in U.S. District Court; if a grievance is taken to the MSPB or to the EEOC and no decision issues within the statutory time limit, the employee may commence an original action in U.S. District Court. 5 U.S.C. §§ 7702(e)(1)&(2).

which employees are given the option of using either (but not both) the contractual grievance and arbitration procedures or certain purely statutory procedures. These issues and options are included in the chart above as Categories II and III (see also Category IV).

The rule concerning "coverage" of the contractual grievance procedure is simple. All grievances are automatically covered by the grievance procedure and can go to arbitration unless excluded by agreement of the parties or unless specifically excluded by statute.[21] Regarding exclusions the statute provides in substance that:[22]

1. Any collective bargaining agreement may exclude any matter from the application of the agreement's grievance procedure.

2. Grievances concerning the following subjects or issues are specifically excluded from the grievance procedure and arbitration: (1) political activities; (2) retirement, life insurance, or health insurance; (3) suspension or removal for national security; (4) examination, certification, or appointment; (5) classification of any position if the classification does not result in the reduction in grade or pay of an employee.

What can qualify as a "grievance" in federal employment? The term "grievance" is defined very broadly as follows:[23]

" 'grievance' means any complaint —

---

may have a statutory MSPB remedy not available to a unit employee. The statute recognizes the right of individual-employee grievance adjustment with representation of the individual's own choosing and with "grievance or appellate rights established" by law, rule, or regulation; except in the case of grievance or appeal procedures negotiated" in the collective agreement. 5 U.S.C. § 7114(a)(5). Even if the collective agreement itself authorizes individual-employee use of the grievance procedure, the authorization may not be broad enough to include all grievances or to include the right to arbitration. For example, see Elmendorf Air Force Base, 71 LA 463, 465-466 (Jackson, 1978). For discussions touching upon the question of a duty of fair representation in the public sector, see PROCEEDINGS OF THE THIRTIETH ANNUAL MEETING OF THE NAA 127-172, 345-346 (The Bureau of National Affairs, Inc., 1978); Note, *Public Sector Grievance Procedures, Due Process, and the Duty of Fair Representation,* 89 HARV. L. REV. 752 (1976).

[21] Concerning the determination of arbitrability of an issue, the fact that the Civil Service Reform Act of 1978 states in 5 U.S.C. § 7121 that collective agreements in the federal sector "shall provide procedures for the settlement of grievances, including questions of arbitrability" indicates that in their agreement the parties are to specify who is to determine arbitrability; presumably questions of arbitrability will be decided by the arbitrator (subject to FLRA review) if the parties do not specify otherwise. However, another provision that may be relevant to the determination of arbitrability in some cases is 5 U.S.C. § 7117(c), which provides that if an agency employer "alleges that the duty to bargain in good faith does not extend to any matter," the union may appeal the allegation to the FLRA under procedures specified in that subsection. Concerning the resolution of federal-sector grievability and arbitrability questions under Executive orders, see Frazier, *Labor Arbitration in the Federal Service,* 45 G.W. L. REV. 712, 750-752 (1977). Also see Social Security Administration, 72 LA 359, 361-362 (Coburn, 1979).

[22] 5 U.S.C. § 7121.

[23] 5 U.S.C. § 7103(a)(9).

(A) by any employee concerning any matter relating to the employment of the employee;

(B) by any labor organization concerning any matter relating to the
employment of any employee; or

(C) by any employee, labor organization, or agency concerning—
    (i) the effect or interpretation, or a claim of breach, of a col-
lective bargaining agreement; or
    (ii) any claimed violation, misinterpretation, or misapplication
of any law, rule, or regulation affecting conditions of employment."

Thus, to reiterate, it is clear (1) that every collective agreement
in the federal sector must provide a grievance procedure and arbitration, (2) that the door to the grievance procedure and arbitration is open wide to all grievances except those specifically excluded
by the agreement or statute, and (3) that the term "grievance" is
defined broadly with the result that an extremely wide variety of
complaints will qualify for access to the grievance procedure and
arbitration. From the viewpoint of the individual employee the
wide open grievance and arbitration door offers the greatest assur-
ance of fair treatment by immediate superiors in accordance with
the collective agreement and governing rules and regulations. This
alone is highly significant.[24]

Scope of Federal-Sector Bargaining and Management-Rights Safeguards

Although the term "grievance" is defined broadly and although the door to the grievance procedure and arbitration may be
wide indeed, strong protection exists against the narrowing of federal agency management right of action and against disregard of
certain laws, rules, and regulations. Both Executive Order 11491
and the Civil Service Reform Act of 1978 contain strong management-rights safeguards. Collective bargaining is prohibited on nu-
merous important matters in the federal sector that are mandatory

---

[24] Illustrating that arbitration can be an effective means for employees to obtain compliance by field offices or installations of a federal agency with regulations of higher level authorities, see U.S. Army Communications Command, 72 LA 44, 45-47 (Leventhal, 1979),
where the agreement itself made regulations of higher level authorities controlling. Also see
Arbitrator Whitman in 69 LA 1097, 1098. In some cases an employee's grievance claim has
been based directly upon a benefit or right claimed under the FEDERAL PERSONNEL MANUAL
or under an agency regulation. See Naval Air Rework Facility, 73 LA 201, 202-203 (Liven-
good, 1979), where the claim was based upon the FPM and the agreement. For an interesting
variation, see Arbitrator Jaffee in 73 LA 138, 141. One arbitrator construed the submission
agreement as confining him to "the four corners" of the collective bargaining agreement; and
although he discussed certain leave benefits for employees under the FPM and agency regulations, he was unwilling to take them into account in reaching his decision, which was that the
collective agreement had not been violated since it did not provide like benefits. Social Security Administration, 72 LA 387, 390-391 (Wahl, 1979). Cf., below, sections entitled "Government-Wide Rules or Regulations" and "Non-Government-Wide Rules or Regulations."

subjects of bargaining in the private sector. Bargaining is merely permitted and not required on certain other important matters in the federal sector that, again, are mandatory subjects of bargaining in the private sector. Nor does the duty to bargain extend to any matter which is the subject of certain rules or regulations. The end result of these prohibitions and limitations is that, although the door to the grievance procedure and arbitration may be open wide, no grievance may properly be sustained in the grievance procedure or arbitration if the grievance stands on a contract provision dealing with a subject excluded from bargaining by statute or if it stands on a contract provision which infringes upon a statutorily safeguarded management right or if sustaining the grievance would infringe upon any of certain laws, rules, or regulations. These matters are treated in the sections that follow.

Management Rights—Prohibited Bargaining Items. "Except as otherwise provided" by Title VII of the Civil Service Reform Act of 1978, federal-sector employees have the right "to engage in collective bargaining with respect to conditions of employment."[25] Bargaining on certain subjects is in effect prohibited by the management-rights section of the Act, which states that "nothing" in Title VII "shall affect the authority of any management official of any agency" (the authority thus being reserved or retained in management):

"(1) to determine the mission, budget, organization, number of employees, and internal security practices of the agency; and

(2) in accordance with applicable laws —

(A) to hire, assign, direct, layoff, and retain employees in the agency, or to suspend, remove, reduce in grade or pay, or take other disciplinary action against such employees;

(B) to assign work, to make determinations with respect to contracting out, and to determine the personnel by which agency operations shall be conducted;

(C) with respect to filling positions, to make selections for appointments from —

(i) among properly ranked and certified candidates for promotion; or

(ii) any other appropriate source; and

---

[25] 5 U.S.C. § 7102. "Collective bargaining" is defined by § 7103(12) to mean "the performance of the mutual obligation of the representative of an agency and the exclusive representative of employees in an appropriate unit in the agency to meet at reasonable times and to consult and bargain in a good-faith effort to reach agreement with respect to the conditions of employment affecting such employees and to execute, if requested by either party, a written document incorporating any collective bargaining agreement reached, but the obligation referred to in this paragraph does not compel either party to agree to a proposal or to make a concession."

(D) to take whatever actions may be necessary to carry out the agency mission during emergencies."[26]

The statutory words "in accordance with applicable laws" do limit management rights, and this limitation would appear to be properly enforceable by contractual grievance and arbitration procedures. Apart from this, however, the statutory reservation of management rights necessarily reduces the scope of grievance-procedure or arbitral authority to disturb actions taken by agency management officials.

It should be noted that in sharp contrast to the general statutory policy of safeguarding management rights in the federal sector, the Postal Reorganization Act's grant of certain specified rights to the Postal Service (similar to the statutory management rights quoted above for federal-sector agencies) is accompanied by significant words of limitation—the Postal Service has the rights *"consistent with . . .* applicable laws, regulations, and *collective-bargaining agreements."* [27]

---

[26] 5 U.S.C. § 7106(a). Illustrating arbitral recognition of the overriding force of federal-sector management rights and the fact that they cannot be bargained away, see Federal Aviation Administration, 68 LA 375, 378-379 (1977), where Arbitrator Richard A. Moore stated that while management rights may be bargained away in the private sector, the federal sector "is a different breed of cat." In considering the Executive Order 11491 counterpart to 5 U.S.C. § 7106(a), he said: "We believe this effectively limits the authority of the Agency to bargain away the matters listed in the section." Executive Order 11491 required collective agreements to contain clauses stating the same management rights stated in the Order itself, as had been done by Article 42 of the agreement before Arbitrator Moore. In this regard, he said: "The Agency's power to bargain is limited by the [Executive order]. It has no authority to bargain away the matters retained in Article 42, Section 2. It follows that other parts of the Agreement should not be interpreted to violate that Article." Also see U.S. Railroad Retirement Board, 71 LA 498, 501, 503 (Sembower, 1978), quoting the FLRC's statement that "implicit and co-extensive with management's conceded authority to decide to take an action under [the Executive Order] is the authority to decide *not* to take such action or to change its decision, once made, whether or not to take such action." Cf., Arbitrator Daly in 72 LA 34, 37, 42-44; Whyte in 70 LA 523, 525-526. It is to be noted that some of the subjects now excluded from bargaining were permissible subjects of bargaining under E.O. 11491. These are mission, budget, organization, number of employees, and internal security practices. On the other hand, another change that may deserve special note is that whereas § 12(b)(5) of E.O. 11491 reserves to management the right to determine the "methods" and "means" by which operations are to be conducted, the "methods" and "means" language does not appear in § 7106(a) but appears rather in § 7106(b) relating to management rights on which bargaining *is* permitted at the election of the federal agency employer (see next section). Illustrating that these words may be an important basis for management action, see National Park Service, 72 LA 314, 322 (Pritzker, 1979). If federal agency management does not elect to bargain on "methods" or "means," it thereby apparently reserves these matters for managerial decision. Another change to be noted is that whereas § 12(b)(4) of E.O. 11491 reserves to management the right "to maintain the efficiency of . . . operations," this has become the 5 U.S.C. § 7101(b) directive that the provisions of the Civil Service Reform Act Title VII, Labor-Management Relations, "should be interpreted in a manner consistent with the requirement of an effective and efficient Government."

[27] 39 U.S.C. § 1001(e), emphasis added. Also indicating the particularly strong status of Postal Service collective agreements, see 39 U.S.C. § 1005(a)(1)(A). For a convincing example of the fact that the Postal Service management rights must be exercised in a manner consist-

Management Rights—Permitted Bargaining Items. The management-rights section's limitation on bargaining subject matter is
qualified, however, by a subsection stating that nothing in the section shall "preclude" any agency and union from negotiating:

> "(1) at the election of the agency, on the numbers, types, and grades
>   of employees or positions assigned to any organizational subdivi-
>   sion, work project, or tour of duty, or on the technology,
>   methods, and means of performing work;
> (2) procedures which management officials of the agency will ob-
>   serve in exercising any authority under this section; or
> (3) appropriate arrangements for employees adversely affected by
>   the exercise of any authority under this section by such manage-
>   ment officials."[28]

The phrase "at the election of the agency" unequivocally applies to
matters listed in paragraph 1 of the subsection, and presumably it
applies also to paragraphs 2 and 3 in view of the introductory statement that nothing shall "preclude" parties from negotiating, a
statement hardly amounting to a mandate for bargaining. Thus,
agency management is permitted but not required to bargain on
the indicated subjects, including *procedures* to be observed by management in exercising its rights and the *impact* upon employees
produced by the exercise of those rights.[29] If federal agency management does bargain on any of these permissible subjects, and if
such bargaining does add provisions to the collective agreement,
the interpretation and application of those provisions would properly fall within the scope of the contractual grievance and arbitration procedures (unless expressly excluded).[30] However, as concerns
those rights on which bargaining is prohibited, "the inclusion of a

---

ent with the collective agreement, and illustrating the broad possibility that the Postal Service
may bargain away management rights, see United States Postal Service, 71 LA 1188,
1195-1197 (Garrett, 1978), where the national collective agreement did effectively impose significant restrictions on management rights.

[28] 5 U.S.C. § 7106(b).

[29] The FLRC under Executive Order 11491 likewise drew a distinction between the exercise of a reserved management right, on the one hand, and the procedures and impact related
thereto (and the FLRC considered bargaining on impact not prohibited). For an excellent
collection and discussion of FLRC decisions outlining the boundaries of prohibited and permitted bargaining under this distinction, see Aronin, *Collective Bargaining in the Federal
Service: A Balanced Approach,* 44 G.W. L. REV. 576, 585-601 (1976). Also, for some relevant arbitration cases under E.O. 11491, see Veterans Administration Medical Center, 72 LA
374, 376 (Sater, 1979); Veterans Administration Hospital, 72 LA 66, 69 (Carson, 1978),
where certain consequences followed upon the employer's exercise of its option by bargaining
on a permissible subject of bargaining under the Executive order. In Marine Corps Develop-
ment Command, 71 LA 726, 730 (Ables, 1978), the Arbitrator appears to have enunciated an
implied limitation on federal-sector management rights.

[30] Illustrating arbitral enforcement of negotiated procedures against federal agency employer's claim of management rights, see Directorate of Supply Operations, 72 LA 1151, 1156
(Daly, 1979).

clause that infringes on a 'retained management right' renders the clause null and void."[31]

Government-Wide Rules or Regulations. Under the Civil Service Reform Act of 1978 the duty to bargain does not extend to any matter which is the subject of any "Government-wide rule or regulation."[32] A savings or "grandfather" clause apparently exists under another section which makes it "an unfair labor practice for an agency . . . to enforce any rule or regulation . . . which is in conflict with any applicable collective bargaining agreement if the agreement was in effect before the date the rule or regulation was prescribed." The one stated exception relates only to discrimination; thus the basic savings clause appears equally applicable to Government-wide and non-Government-wide rules and regulations.[33]

The phrase "Government-wide rule or regulation" refers basically to rules and regulations contained in the *Federal Personnel Manual* (FPM). The source and role of the *Federal Personnel Manual* has been explained as follows:

> "The laws governing the personnel policies of federal employees are pervasive. Title 5 of the United States Code covers such matters as pay, fringe benefits, classifications, performance ratings, and incentive awards. In addition, Congress has authorized the [Civil Service] Commission to promulgate regulations implementing most of the legislation on federal personnel policies. Pursuant to statute, the President has authority to prescribe regulations for the conduct of employees in the executive branch. These laws and regulations have been compiled in the FPM, which Executive Order 11,491 excludes from the scope of collective bargaining."[34]

Thus we have seen that under both the Civil Service Reform Act of 1978 and Executive Order 11491 the subject matter contained in the FPM is excluded from mandatory bargaining. Moreover, where

---

[31] Tobias, *The Scope of Bargaining in the Federal Sector: Collective Bargaining or Collective Consultation,* 44 G.W. L. REV. 554, 557 (1976), citing FLRC decisions.

[32] 5 U.S.C. § 7117(a)(1). Also relevant is § 7103(a)(14). Under the Act collective agreements are subject to approval by the agency head within 30 days after execution of the agreement in order to review compliance with "applicable law, rule, or regulation." 5 U.S.C. § 7114(c)(1)&(2).

[33] 5 U.S.C. § 7116(a)(7). For application of a related savings provision under Executive orders, see Southwest Power Administration, 72 LA 31, 32, 34 (Schedler, 1978).

[34] Tobias, *The Scope of Bargaining in the Federal Sector: Collective Bargaining or Collective Consultation,* 44 G.W. L. REV. 554, 555-556 (1976). The former Civil Service Commission's function of maintaining and updating the FPM (which comprises ten or more volumes) is now shared by the OPM, the MSPB, and the FLRA, each in its respective area of operations. The sheer bulk of the FPM and other regulation handbooks may leave an arbitrator at least momentarily appalled. See U.S. Dept. of HUD, 69 LA 961, 961-962 (Comey, 1977).

as a result of voluntary bargaining or otherwise the FPM and a collective agreement provision conflict, the FPM controls.[35]

Consultation Rights. Although the duty to bargain does not apply to any matter which is the subject of any "Government-wide rule or regulation," the statute does provide, apparently in reference to agencies which issue Government-wide rules and regulations, that the union "shall be granted consultation rights by any agency with respect to any Government-wide rule or regulation issued by the agency affecting any substantive change in any condition of employment."[36] A union's statutory consultation rights include the right to receive advance notice of proposed changes in conditions of employment, opportunity to present views and recommendations, agency obligation to consider such views and recommendations before taking final action and to give the union a written statement of the reasons for taking the final action.[37] Executive Order 11491 also specified consultation rather than bargaining rights for some matters. One critic concluded that it excessively limited the issues subject to bargaining, leaving "only the right of consultation concerning many of the vital conditions of employment."[38] However, a Civil Service Commission official stressed that it should not be concluded from the limitations on the scope of federal-sector bargaining that the content of negotiated agreements had been meaningless, and he offered a sizeable list of important matters that had been negotiated.[39]

---

[35] It was stressed by the FLRC under Executive Order 11491 that "Arbitrators should consider appropriate regulations, such as those in the Federal Personnel Manual, and ensure that their awards are consistent with them." Frazier, *Labor Arbitration in the Federal Service*, 45 G.W. L. REV. 712, 733 (1977). Illustrating the overriding authority of the FPM as a limitation upon federal agency collective bargaining, and illustrating an arbitrator's alertness to the fact that disregard of that authority renders the award vulnerable "as an abuse of the Arbitrator's [own] authority," see General Services Administration, 71 LA 860, 864 (Leeper, 1978). The obligation to consider regulations may require the arbitrator to interpret and determine the scope of the regulations. See, for instance, Internal Revenue Service, 71 LA 1018, 1019-1020 (Harkless, 1978). The FPM and other regulations cited by a federal agency employer did not control where they were construed not to be directly applicable to the narrow issue before the arbitrator; literal language of the agreement covered the issue and the arbitrator stated that "the parties are obligated to live with its literal meaning to the extent it is not inconsistent with existing laws or regulations." Patent and Trademark Office, 71 LA 39, 41-42 (Gentry, 1978). In another case the FPM provisions relied upon by the employer were found to be "nondispositive" of the issue before the arbitrator, whereas past practice of the parties was clear and controlling. Norfolk Naval Shipyard, 72 LA 364, 365-366 (Moran, 1979).

[36] 5 U.S.C. § 7117(d)(1). Also dealing with consultation rights, see § 7113.

[37] 5 U.S.C. § 7117(d)(2)&(3).

[38] Tobias, *The Scope of Bargaining in the Federal Sector: Collective Bargaining or Collective Consultation*, 44 G.W. L. REV. 554, 555 (1976). Illustrating that (contractual) consultation rights may be inadequate from the viewpoint of employees, see Social Security Administration, 70 LA 699, 700-701 (Atleson, 1978), where the agreement drew a distinction between the obligation to "confer" and the obligation to "consult."

[39] Aronin, *Collective Bargaining in the Federal Service: A Balanced Approach*, 44 G.W.

Non-Government-Wide Rules or Regulations.[40] No general "yes" or "no" answer is available for the question of whether the duty to bargain under the Civil Service Reform Act of 1978 extends to matters which are the subject of any non-Government-wide rule or regulation or for the related question of whether a non-Government-wide rule or regulation will control over a conflicting collective agreement provision. Rather, the answer to these questions appears to depend upon (1) the agency level at which the rule or regulation is issued, (2) the level and scope of the bargaining unit which has produced the collective agreement provision, and (3) in certain situations, an FLRA determination that "no compelling need" exists for the rule or regulation.

The substance of two directly relevant statutory subsections construed together is that the duty to bargain extends to matters which are the subject of any rule or regulation "issued by any agency or issued by any primary national subdivision of such agency" if, but "only if," the FLRA has determined that "no compelling need (as determined under regulations prescribed by the Authority) exists for the rule or regulation."[41] However, the statute states an exception. The "no compelling need" finding must be made as a condition precedent to any duty to bargain, "unless an exclusive representative represents an appropriate unit including not less than a majority of the employees in the issuing agency or primary national subdivision, as the case may be, to whom the rule or regulation is applicable."[42]

L. REV. 576, 602 (1976), stating that: "Within the limitations [on the scope of bargaining], parties have negotiated merit promotion procedures, evaluation procedures, evaluation criteria to be used in promotions, and union participation on promotion panels. They have negotiated on environmental pay differentials, overtime distribution, and procedures relating to assignments. Negotiated agreements contain provisions relating to all matters of health and safety, to equal employment opportunity, and to leave administration. Working rules, codes of discipline, and performance standards have been established. These agreements provide for employee facilities, parking spaces, reimbursement for travel, and, most important, comprehensive grievance systems with binding arbitration."

[40] As used in this material, the term "non-Government-wide" refers to Government rules and regulations which are not Government-wide in application.

[41] 5 U.S.C. § 7117(a)(2)&(3). Also relevant is § 7103(a)(14). Section 7117(b) specifies detailed procedures, to be expedited to the extent practicable, for obtaining an FLRA determination regarding compelling need. Executive Order 11491 also made "compelling need" a controlling factor. One authority explained that under criteria adopted by the FLRC, "regulations may bar negotiations below the level of issuance only if issued at the agency headquarters level or at the level of a primary national subdivision and if they meet the criteria issued by the Council." Aronin, *Collective Bargaining in the Federal Service: A Balanced Approach,* 44 G.W. L. REV. 576, 601 (1976), where it is also stated that: "These criteria require that before any published personnel policy can bar negotiations below the level of issuance, the policy must be essential to the agency's mission or management, required for the protection of merit principles, mandated by a nondiscretionary policy issued outside the agency, or designed to achieve uniformity in personnel policies over a substantial segment of the agency."

[42] 5 U.S.C. § 7117(a)(3). Also relevant is § 7103(a)(14).

The statute does not state any limitation upon the duty to bargain on matters which are the subject of any rule or regulation issued below the level of primary national subdivision of an agency. It thus appears clear that rules and regulations issued at such lower levels of an agency have a status at the opposite extreme from that of Government-wide rules or regulations. That is, there is a duty to bargain on matters (assuming they are otherwise proper subjects for bargaining) which are the subject only of a rule or regulation issued below the level of primary national subdivision of an agency; and a collective agreement provision would control over such lower level rules or regulations where they conflict.

Between the two extremes stand those rules and regulations "issued by any agency [no doubt this means issued at the top level or headquarters of the agency] or issued by any primary national subdivision of such agency." For ready reference, these may be termed "intermediate" rules and regulations as distinguished from "Government-wide" rules and regulations or from "lower level" rules and regulations issued below the level of primary national subdivision of an agency.

As noted above, the duty to bargain extends to matters which are the subject of any "intermediate" rule or regulation only if the FLRA has determined that "no compelling need" exists for the rule or regulation, or if, under the statutory exception, the union "represents an appropriate unit including not less than a majority of the employees in the issuing agency or primary national subdivision, as the case may be, to whom the rule or regulation is applicable." It appears that the following results are produced by this statutory scheme:

1. A rule or regulation issued at the top level or headquarters of an agency, or issued by any primary national subdivision of the agency, will control over any conflicting collective agreement negotiated below the primary national subdivision level unless the FLRA has determined that "no compelling need" exists for the rule or regulation; if the FLRA has made such determination, the collective agreement will control.[43]

---

[43] On the basis of a 1978 statistical summary it appears likely that the great bulk of federal-sector bargaining units exist at a level below the primary national subdivision level. The statistics reveal that within 83 national agencies in the federal sector there were 2,233 collective agreements for 2,609 "Recognitions Covered." UNION RECOGNITION IN THE FEDERAL GOVERNMENT 20-21 (Office of Personnel Management, OLMR-79-03). The statistics identify 87 unions holding federal-sector representation rights (44 are independent unions and the others are AFL unions). Id. at 22-23.

2. A rule or regulation issued at the top level or headquarters of an agency, or issued by any primary national subdivision of the agency, will not control over any conflicting collective agreement if the agreement was negotiated by a union which "represents an appropriate unit including not less than a majority of the employees in the issuing agency or primary national subdivision, as the case may be, to whom the rule or regulation is applicable."

The policy underlying this statutory scheme is both obvious and reasonable. At the upper levels of the agency, where top management makes the bargaining judgments with a union speaking for at least a large segment of the agency's employees, the union has a statutory right to bargain (assuming the matter is otherwise a proper subject for bargaining) without regard to the agency's rules and regulations; and those rules and regulations will not control over the collective agreement if they conflict. On the other hand, stability of agency operations and management-employee relations as well requires that rules and regulations issued at upper levels for broad application and for which "compelling need" exists must control over conflicting collective agreements negotiated by the agency's lower level bargaining units.[44] Meanwhile, at opposite extremes, justification is equally strong (1) for not permitting collective agreements to prevail against a rule or regulation issued for "Government-wide" application, but (2) for permitting collective agreements to prevail against a rule or regulation issued at lower levels of an agency, applying only at the limited "local" level and concerning matters appropriate for local determination.

Review of Arbitration Awards

All arbitration awards in the federal sector are subject to some type of review. The "Processing Channels" chart provided above indicates categories of issues and the processing channels for each category. If a grievance does not involve any adverse-action issue listed under Category II, and does not involve any discrimination issue, an arbitration award resolving the grievance is subject to review only by the Federal Labor Relations Authority as indicated in the Category I segment of the chart (and the FLRA decision is final unless an unfair labor practice issue is involved). No doubt a

---

[44] Similar considerations may underlie the general dominance of a master agreement over a local agreement in the federal sector. See Bureau of Prisons, 73 LA 435 (Fitch, 1979), dealing with the relationship between a master agreement negotiated at the national level and agreements negotiated at the local level.

high percentage of all federal-sector grievances will fall into Category I. Thus for many arbitration awards the only possibility for review will be by the FLRA (but what the FLRA ultimately does in its review may be significantly affected by the related role and actions of the Comptroller General[45]). In addition, the FLRA has an intermediate review role for awards involving discrimination issues, provided no Category II issue is also involved.

The remainder of this section deals only with the FLRA review, and the reader is directed to the aforementioned chart for other tribunals with review functions where a Category II, III, or IV grievance is involved.

Under the Civil Service Reform Act of 1978 either party may file exceptions to any arbitration award with the FLRA (unless the award involves any issue listed under Category II of the chart above). After so providing, the statute continues:[46]

> "If upon review the Authority finds that the award is deficient —
>   (1) because it is contrary to any law, rule, or regulation; or
>   (2) on other grounds similar to those applied by Federal courts in private sector labor-management relations;
> the Authority may take such action and make such recommendations concerning the award as it considers necessary, consistent with applicable laws, rules, or regulations.

> "(b) If no exception to an arbitrator's award is filed under subsection (a) of this section during the 30-day period beginning on the date of such award, the award shall be final and binding. An agency shall take the actions required by an arbitrator's final award. The award may include the payment of backpay (as provided in section 5596 of this title)."

The foregoing statutory grounds for review are essentially a codification of the review grounds adopted by the Federal Labor Relations Council under Executive Order 11491, which did not state grounds but authorized the Council to do so. The Council adopted the following grounds for review:[47]

---

[45] See the next section entitled "Comptroller General's Review Role." The federal agency's compliance with the arbitrator's award may similarly be affected.

[46] 5 U.S.C. § 7122(a). The fact that exceptions to the award can be filed may result in expanded coverage of the facts and parties' positions in the federal-sector arbitrator's written opinion. An illustration is San Antonio Air Logistics Center, 73 LA 455, 463 (LeBaron, 1979).

[47] Frazier, *Labor Arbitration in the Federal Sector*, 45 G.W. L. REV. 712, 717-750 (1977), where decisions are cited to illustrate the scope and application of the grounds for review. Also see discussion by Gamser, *Back-Seat Driving Behind the Back-Seat Driver: Arbitration in the Federal Sector*, PROCEEDINGS OF THE THIRTY-FIRST ANNUAL MEETING OF NAA (The Bureau of National Affairs, Inc., 1979), pp. 268, 273-276, indicating 15 percent of federal-sector awards had been appealed to the FLRC, a significantly higher rate of appeals than in the private sector. For a comprehensive survey of federal-sector arbitration decisions and FLRC disposition of those reviewed, see the publication of U.S. Civil Service Commission Of-

1. The award violates applicable law.
2. The award violates an "appropriate regulation."
3. The award violates Executive Order 11491.[48]

Additionally, the Council adopted the following grounds, said to be "similar to those on which courts sustain challenges to arbitration awards in the private sector":

1. The arbitrator exceeded his authority.
2. The award does not draw its essence from the collective bargaining agreement.
3. The award is incomplete, ambiguous, or contradictory, making implementation of the award impossible.
4. The award is based on a "nonfact."
5. The arbitrator was biased or partial.
6. The arbitrator refused to hear pertinent and material evidence.

The Council's executive director believed that the "value and strength of labor dispute arbitration depend upon the finality of the arbitrator's decision" and that "courts and agencies authorized to review the decision must be reluctant to interfere with it."[49] He summed up the teaching of Council reports and decisions:

> "As in the private sector, federal sector arbitration is a creation of the parties and their collective bargaining agreement. The Council has emphasized, through its reports and decisions, that it will intervene in the arbitration process only to the limited extent that an award comes within one of the Council's grounds for review. The Council patterned its philosophy of limited review in large part on that in the private sector. The Council also recognizes, as do courts in the private sector, that arbitrators need leeway in formulating remedies. In the federal sector, however, arbitrators must take into account and act consistently with applicable federal laws, appropriate regulations, and the [Executive] Order."[50]

---

fice of Labor-Management Relations entitled GRIEVANCE ARBITRATION IN THE FEDERAL SERVICE (PRINCIPLES, PRACTICES AND PRECEDENTS), issued in 1977 and for sale by the National Technical Information Service, Dept. of Commerce, Springfield, Virginia 22161.

[48] For example, "an award may not erode rights designed to protect the public interest that are reserved to management by the Order." Frazier, *Labor Arbitration in the Federal Sector*, 45 G.W. L. REV. 712, 734 (1977).

[49] Id. at 721.

[50] Id. at 755-756. "[The cases] illustrate a basic difference between private sector and federal sector arbitration. In the private sector, the negotiated terms of the collective bargaining agreement govern the resolution of grievances. Arbitrators in the federal sector, however, must consider not only the terms of the parties' agreement, but also the provisions of statutes and regulations that may apply to the grievance with which they are presented. Federal sector agencies and unions are generally more aware than arbitrators of statutes and regulations applicable in a given situation and should advise arbitrators of the statutes and regulations that might apply to a particular grievance." Id. at 730.

General continuation of the Council's limited review policy by the Council's successor, the Federal Labor Relations Authority, is indicated by statements of the FLRA Director of Arbitration Services.[51] That speaker stated that awards have not been and will not be overturned merely because of disagreement with the arbitrator's findings of fact, reasoning and conclusion, or conclusions drawn from the evidence. However, he reminded that in the vast majority of instances in which the Council had set aside or modified an award, it was done on the ground that the award violated applicable law or a Government-wide regulation, and he cautioned that: (1) the federal-sector arbitrator must consider and conform to relevant laws and regulations in deciding cases and formulating remedies — primarily the provisions of Title 5 of the United States Code and the rules and regulations contained in the *Federal Personnel Manual;* (2) the parties have an obligation to bring relevant laws and regulations to the arbitrator's attention, and the arbitrator should request it if they have not done so; (3) in many instances the critical review area concerns the remedy directed by the arbitrator and its conformance with law and regulation. Regarding these caveats, the role of the Comptroller General also must be considered.

Comptroller General's Review Role

The right and responsibility of the Comptroller General to review awards issued in federal-sector arbitration during the period of Executive order programs was explained by that official in a 1977 General Accounting Office publication as follows:

> "The Comptroller General has a statutory responsibility to review awards in which agency officials question the propriety of Federal expenditures ordered by a third party. Under 31 U.S.C. 74 and 82(d), disbursing officers, certifying officers, and heads of Government departments or establishments have the right to apply for and obtain advance decisions from the Comptroller General on any question of law involved in the expenditure of Federal funds, including those ordered by a binding arbitration award, Assistant Secretary of Labor decision, or Federal Labor Relations Council decision."[52]

---

[51] Transcript of Discussion on Problems of Arbitration in the Federal Sector (N.A.A., 1979). The discussion occurred on December 29, 1978; and the transcript was disseminated for discussion purposes only by the National Academy of Arbitrators Subcommittee on Seminars.

[52] The quoted statement appears on the cover of the MANUAL ON REMEDIES AVAILABLE TO THIRD PARTIES IN ADJUDICATING FEDERAL EMPLOYEE GRIEVANCES. There is also stated that "GAO prepared this manual to assist third parties in fashioning remedies consistent with Federal statutes and regulations," and that the manual "details the available remedies for the most common cases requiring make-whole remedies." The foreword states GAO plans "to up-

Comptroller General views and actions in reviewing federal-sector arbitration awards have sometimes been strongly criticized. It has been charged that the Comptroller General "has directly involved himself in the determination of the merits" of some cases and that his decisions "thus pose a difficult obstacle if arbitration is to be an effective process in federal labor relations."[53] Another critic declared that the "Comptroller General has constricted the scope of bargaining beyond the limitations designated by the FLRC" and has "undermined [the federal-sector] arbitration process by accepting agency appeals from arbitration awards in direct conflict with FLRC rulings." This critic urged that statutory reforms "should eliminate entirely [the Comptroller General's] role in federal labor relations."[54]

The Federal Labor Relations Council sometimes requested rulings from the Comptroller General, and its acknowledgment of the authority of Comptroller General rulings was reflected in the FLRC executive director's comments concerning Comptroller General application of the Back Pay Act of 1966 to federal agency violations of collective agreements—comments which also underscore the "but for" test or limitation upon the remedy power of federal-sector arbitrators:

> "Overruling his previous decisions to the contrary, the Comptroller General declared [in his 1974 "NLRB" decision] that the Back Pay Act was appropriate statutory authority for compensating the employee for pay, allowances, or differentials he would have received *but for* violation of the agreement.
>
> "In accordance with the Comptroller General's interpretation of the Back Pay Act in NLRB and subsequent decisions, the Council has upheld backpay awards which met NLRB requirements, including

---

date the manual as changes in laws, appropriate regulations, and Comptroller General decisions occur." Copies of the manual may be obtained by writing to U.S. General Accounting Office, Distribution Section Room 4522, 441 G Street, N.W., Washington, D.C. 20548.

[53] Kagel, *Grievance Arbitration in the Federal Service: How Final and Binding?*, 51 OREGON L. REV. 134, 148-149 (1971). For similar criticism see Gamser, *Back-Seat Driving Behind the Back-Seat Driver: Arbitration in the Federal Sector*, PROCEEDINGS OF THE THIRTY-FIRST ANNUAL MEETING OF NAA (The Bureau of National Affairs, Inc., 1979), pp. 268, 276-279; Porter, *Arbitration in the Federal Government: What Happened to the 'Magna Carta'?* PROCEEDINGS OF THE THIRTIETH ANNUAL MEETING OF NAA (The Bureau of National Affairs, Inc., 1978), pp. 90, 98-102.

[54] Tobias, *The Scope of Bargaining in the Federal Sector: Collective Bargaining or Collective Consultation*, 44 G.W. L. REV. 554, 570-572 (1976). Regarding his first point Tobias explained that under the authority to review requests concerning expenditure of government funds, the Comptroller General "reserves the right to review clauses in collective bargaining agreements and declare them null and void." Regarding his second point Tobias quoted the Comptroller General's statement [54 Comp. Gen. 921, 927 (1975)] that whether the agency "does or does not file [exceptions to an arbitration award] with the Council the agency at any time has the right to request a decision of the Comptroller General in matters relating to the expenditure of Government funds," and the Comptroller General's decision "is binding on the agency, the Council and the Assistant Secretary of Labor." Id. at 557, 572.

the *but for* test. In some situations, however, notably 'failure to consult' cases, a grievant is unlikely to satisfy the *but for* standard."[55] Arbitrators, too, have given careful attention to Comptroller General decisions in order to satisfy themselves that their awards are not inconsistent with that Official's views.[56]

Contrary to the urging of some critics, Congress did not eliminate the Comptroller General's role in labor relations when the Civil Service Reform Act of 1978 was enacted. Indeed, Congress now gave the Comptroller General express statutory authority to "conduct audits and reviews to assure compliance with the laws, rules, and regulations governing employment" in the federal sector.[57]

Nonetheless, other provisions of the Civil Service Reform Act possibly will affect the role and actions of the Comptroller General in connection with review of federal-sector arbitration awards:

1. The statute now expressly provides that an arbitrator's award "shall be final and binding" if no exceptions are filed with the FLRA within 30 days, and that the agency "shall take the actions required by an arbitrator's final award."[58]

2. The statute now expressly provides that an arbitrator's award "may include the payment of backpay" as provided by the Back Pay Act, and the Back Pay Act was amended making it expressly applicable in the disposition of grievances under collective agreements (see the section below entitled "The Back Pay Act").[59]

---

[55] Frazier, *Labor Arbitration in the Federal Service*, 45 G.W. L. REV. 712, 723 (1977). Also dealing with application of the "but for" test or limitation upon arbitral remedy power, see Ferris, *Remedies in Federal Sector Promotion Grievances*, 34 ARB. J. 37 (1979). The Back Pay Act specifies back pay for employees "affected by an unjustified or unwarranted personnel action which has resulted in the withdrawal or reduction of all or part of the pay, allowances, or differentials of the employee." The Comptroller General's MANUAL ON REMEDIES, Appendix I, stresses that the employee's loss must have resulted "directly" from the unjustified or unwarranted personnel action (an interpretation which in effect interpolates the word "directly" into the statute), and the manual states the "but for" requirement as follows: "A direct causal relationship must be established between the unjustified or unwarranted personnel action and the loss of pay, allowances, or differentials. Remedies under the Back Pay Act are not available unless it is established that 'but for' the wrongful action, the withdrawal of pay, allowances, or differentials would not have occurred." Although the Back Pay Act was amended by the Civil Service Reform Act of 1978, no change was made in the above-quoted language on which the Comptroller General's "but for" test is based. Since that critical language was not changed, the Comptroller General may not be inclined to moderate his strict insistence that the "but for" finding be made and demonstrated in order to support an arbitrator's award of back pay.

[56] See Arbitrator Keltner in 73 LA 429, 432-433, 435; Wahl in 72 LA 1044, 1046; Robertson in 71 LA 869, 872; Merrifield in 70 LA 365, 368. Also see Arbitrator Kaplan in 69 LA 1149, 1150 fn. 1, 1153.

[57] 5 U.S.C. § 2304. For additional authority given the Comptroller General under this statute, see, above, the section entitled *"General Accounting Office* (GAO)."

[58] 5 U.S.C. § 7122(b). Does this present a conflict with Comptroller General authority under 31 U.S.C. §§ 74, 82(d), or under the above-noted language of 5 U.S.C. § 2304?

[59] 5 U.S.C. §§ 5596, 7122(b). As noted above, however, the Back Pay Act language on

3. The statute provides that FLRA may request from OPM "an advisory opinion concerning the proper interpretation of rules, regulations, or policy directives issued by the Office of Personnel Management in connection with any matter before the Authority."[60]

The Back Pay Act

The Back Pay Act of 1966 was amended in 1978 to make it expressly applicable in the disposition of grievances under collective bargaining agreements. In view of its significance to the arbitrator's remedy power, the following subsection of the Act is reproduced here for the reader:[61]

"(b) (1) An employee of an agency who, on the basis of a timely appeal or an administrative determination (including a decision relating to an unfair labor practice or a grievance) is found by appropriate authority under applicable law, rule, regulation, or collective bargaining agreement, to have been affected by an unjustified or unwarranted personnel action which has resulted in the withdrawal or reduction of all or part of the pay, allowances, or differentials of the employee—
(A) is entitled, on correction of the personnel action, to receive for the period for which the personnel action was in effect—
(i) an amount equal to all or any part of the pay, allowances, or differentials, as applicable which the employee normally would have earned or received during the period if the personnel action had not occurred, less any amounts earned by the employee through other employment during that period; and
(ii) reasonable attorney fees related to the personnel action which, with respect to any decision relating to an unfair labor practice or a grievance processed under a procedure negotiated in accordance with chapter 71 of this title, shall be awarded in accordance with standards established under section 7701(g) of this title; and
(B) [Here it is provided that annual leave in excess of the maximum leave accumulation permitted by law shall be credited to a separate leave account for the employee who has undergone an unjustified or unwarranted personnel action that has caused annual leave loss.]
(2) This subsection does not apply to any reclassification action nor authorize the setting aside of an otherwise proper promotion by a selecting official from a group of properly ranked and certified candidates.

which the Comptroller General's strict "but for" interpretation has been based was not changed, and that official may not be inclined to moderate his interpretation of the language.
[60] 5 U.S.C. § 7105(i). Although this arguably produces an implied exclusion or limitation of the Comptroller General's role, it would seem that an express provision would be required for that result.
[61] 5 U.S.C. § 5596(b).

(3) For the purpose of this subsection, "grievance" and "collective bargaining agreement" have the meanings set forth in section 7103 of this title, "unfair labor practice" means an unfair labor practice described in section 7116 of this title, and "personnel action" includes the omission or failure to take an action or confer a benefit."

The statutory provision for "reasonable attorney fees" applies where the employee is the prevailing party and payment of attorney fees by the agency "is warranted in the interest of justice, including any case in which a prohibited personnel practice was engaged in by the agency or any case in which the agency's action was clearly without merit."[62]

A Recapitulation From the Arbitrator's Viewpoint

It would appear from foregoing materials that the federal-sector arbitrator's task is to enforce the collective bargaining agreement and decide the grievance on the basis of the agreement, *unless*

1. The grievance involves one of the matters specifically excluded from the grievance procedure and arbitration by statute or by the parties themselves; or
2. The collective agreement contravenes a management right which is excluded from bargaining by statute or one on which management is permitted but not required to bargain (and management has elected not to bargain); or
3. The collective agreement contravenes an applicable law or a "Government-wide" rule or regulation; or contravenes a rule or regulation issued at the top level or headquarters of an agency or issued by any primary national subdivision of an agency, unless the FLRA has determined that "no compelling need" exists for the rule or regulation, or unless the collective agreement was negotiated by a union which "represents an appropriate unit including not less than a majority of the employees in the issuing agency or primary national subdivision, as the case may be, to whom the rule or regulation is applicable."

Finally, in the event of a sustaining award the arbitrator's remedy should comport with and meet any limitations imposed by the Back Pay Act and any other controlling law, rule, or regulation.

---

[62] 5 U.S.C. § 7701(g), the stated basis for awarding attorney fees applying also to MSPB decisions. The Comptroller General's MANUAL ON REMEDIES takes the position that punitive damages may not be awarded, and that this is true also of interest on backpay since the statute does not authorize interest.

Topical Index

A

Age discrimination (See Discrimination)
Agreements (See Collective bargaining agreements)
Annual leave 25
Appeals (See also names of U.S. courts)
  Back Pay Act applicability 25, 26
  Merit Systems Protection Board functions 3, 8, 9
  rate of 20n.
Arbitrability
  collective bargaining agreements scope 7, 10n.
  federal versus private sector arbitrability 1
  awards
    appeals rate 20n.
    attorney fees 25, 26
    back pay 20, 25, 26
    Federal Labor Relations Authority role 5
    personnel laws consideration 16n.
    review of 19 et seq.
  federal and private sector comparison 1, 13n., 21
  grievance-processing channels 6, 8, 9
  legal status 1 et seq.
  procedural changes 2
  role and scope 6 et seq., 26
Arbitrators
  arbitration awards review criteria 21
  personnel laws consideration 16n.
  scope of authority 1, 26
Army Communications Command 11n.
Attorney fees 25, 26
Awards (See Arbitration, awards)

B

Back pay
  arbitration awards 20, 25, 26
  interest on 26n.
Back Pay Act of 1966
  applicability to grievance dispositions 25, 26

Comptroller General's interpretation of 23, 24
Bureau of Prisons 19n.

C

Civil Rights Act of 1964 (See also Discrimination) 3, 5
Civil Service Commission (See also Merit Systems Protection Board; Office of Personnel Management)
  functions prior to termination 3, 15n.
  functions transfer 3, 4
Civil Service Reform Act of 1978
  arbitration awards appeals provisions 20
  Back Pay Act amendments 25, 26
  changes made by 2 et seq.
  collective bargaining agreements scope 10n.
  "grandfather" clause 15
  management bargaining obligations and rights 11 et seq.
Claims Court (See U.S. Court of Claims)
Complaints (See Grievance procedures)
Comptroller General (See General Accounting Office)
Collective bargaining
  definition of 12n.
  duty to bargain, scope/limitations of 5, 11 et seq.
  Federal Labor Relations Authority jurisdiction 5
  negotiation impasses, resolution of 2, 3, 6
  permitted bargaining items 14, 15
  prohibited bargaining items 12, 13
Collective bargaining agreements
  arbitration awards review criteria 21
  Back Pay Act applicability 25, 26
  enforcement exceptions 10, 11, 26
  government regulations, conflicts with 15 et seq., 26
  grievance procedures, inclusion 7, 10, 11
  management rights relative to 13, 14, 15, 26

27

BNA Publications on Arbitration

Books

Anatomy of a Labor Arbitration (1961)
by Sam Kagel
   A "how-to-do-it" book on the preparation and presentation of grievance arbitration.   ISBN 0-87179-025-4 $10.00

Arbitration and Labor Relations (3rd Edition, 1970)
by Clarence M. Updegraff
   A practical yet scholarly book concerned with the procedural and substantive aspects of labor arbitration.   ISBN 0-87179-098-X $15.00

The Arbitration of Industrial Engineering Disputes (1970)
by Ronald L. Wiggins
   Presents the first comprehensive study of industrial engineering disputes involving the relationships between the work employees do and the wages they are paid. The author identifies the principles that arbitrators apply in resolving disputes and explores the qualifications of arbitrators selected to settle industrial engineering disputes.   ISBN 0-87179-106-4 $12.50

How Arbitration Works (3rd Edition, 1973; 4th Edition in preparation)
by Frank Elkouri and Edna Asper Elkouri
   A standard work in the field of labor arbitration since it was first published in 1952. This book's clear, logical, and orderly presentation enables the reader to turn quickly to the problem area and grasp the issues involved.
                                ISBN 0-87179-180-3 $17.50

Practice and Procedure in Labor Arbitration (1973)
by Owen Fairweather
   Discusses significant aspects of the labor arbitration process, from initial submission to post-hearing procedure, in the light of the applicable statutory and decisional law, concentrating on procedural questions and problems.
                                ISBN 0-87179-188-9 $25.00

Preparing and Presenting Your Arbitration Case (1979)
by Allan J. Harrison
   This brief, practical manual stresses the need for sound preparation of evidence and arguments prior to the arbitration hearing.   ISBN 0-87179-303-2 $4.00

Proceedings of the Annual Meetings of the National Academy of Arbitrators, 1948-1979 $20.00 each

Proving Your Arbitration Case (1961)
by Boaz Siegel
   This pamphlet examines the application of rules of evidence to labor arbitration cases.   ISBN 0-87179-087-4 $1.50

Services

Labor Arbitration Reports
   Provides weekly reports on awards and recommended settlements by arbitrators, emergency boards, factfinding bodies, permanent referees, and umpires. Reports on company and union positions, dissenting opinions. Gives biographical directories of arbitrators and references to published decisions. Indexed, with Table of Cases.

The Bureau of National Affairs, Inc.
1231 25th Street, N.W., Washington, D.C. 20037
Telephone: (202) 452-4200

I'm going to read

UP TO
50
WORDS

I'm Going To READ!™

These levels are meant only as guides;
you and your child can best choose a book that's right.

Level 1: Kindergarten–Grade 1 . . . Ages 4–6
- word bank to highlight new words
- consistent placement of text to promote readability
- easy words and phrases
- simple sentences build to make simple stories
- art and design help new readers decode text

Level 2: Grade 1 . . . Ages 6–7
- word bank to highlight new words
- rhyming texts introduced
- more difficult words, but vocabulary is still limited
- longer sentences and longer stories
- designed for easy readability

Level 3: Grade 2 . . . Ages 7–8
- richer vocabulary of up to 200 different words
- varied sentence structure
- high-interest stories with longer plots
- designed to promote independent reading

Level 4: Grades 3 and up . . . Ages 8 and up
- richer vocabulary of more than 300 different words
- short chapters, multiple stories, or poems
- more complex plots for the newly independent reader
- emphasis on reading for meaning

Note to Parents

What a great sense of achievement it is when you can accomplish a goal! With the **I'm Going To Read!**™series, goals are established when you pick up a book. This series was developed to grow with the new reader. The vocabulary grows quantifiably from 50 different words at Level One, to 100 different words at Level Two, to 200 different words at Level Three, and to 300 different words at Level Four.

Ways to Use the Word Bank

- Read along with your child and help him or her sound out the words in the word bank.

- Have your child find the word in the word bank as you read it aloud.

- Ask your child to find the word in the word bank that matches a picture on the page.

- Review the words in the word bank and then ask your child to read the story to you.

Related Word Bank Activities

- Create mini-flash cards in your handwriting. This provides yet another opportunity for the reader to be able to identify words, regardless of what the typography looks like.

- Think of a sentence and then place the mini-flash cards on a table out of order. Ask your child to rearrange the mini-flash cards until the sentence makes sense.

- Make up riddles about words in the story and have your child find the appropriate mini-flash card. For example, "It's red and it bounces. What is it?"

- Choose one of the mini-flash cards and ask your child to find the same word in the text of the story.

- Create a second set of mini-flash cards and play a game of Concentration, trying to match the pairs of words.

LEVEL 1

STERLING CHILDREN'S BOOKS
New York

An Imprint of Sterling Publishing
387 Park Avenue South
New York, NY 10016

Lot: 14   16   18   20   19   17   15   13   02/14

Published by Sterling Publishing Co., Inc.
387 Park Avenue South, New York, NY 10016
Text copyright © 2005 by Harriet Ziefert Inc.
Illustrations copyright © 2005 by Carol Nicklaus
Distributed in Canada by Sterling Publishing
c/o Canadian Manda Group, 165 Dufferin Street
Toronto, Ontario, Canada M6K 3H6
Distributed in the United Kingdom by GMC Distribution Services,
Castle Place, 166 High Street, Lewes, East Sussex, England BN7 1XU
Distributed in Australia by Capricorn Link (Australia) Pty. Ltd.
P.O. Box 704, Windsor, NSW 2756, Australia

I'm Going To Read is a trademark of Sterling Publishing Co., Inc.

Sterling ISBN-13: 978-1-4027-2090-1

For information about custom editions, special sales, premium and
corporate purchases, please contact Sterling Special Sales
Department at 800-805-5489 or specialsales@sterlingpub.com.

Sometimes
I Share

Pictures by Carol Nicklaus

STERLING CHILDREN'S BOOKS
New York

Sometimes I share.

my   give   cookie

Sometimes I give my brother
half of my cookie.

Sometimes I let my brother
play with my toys.

bike

Sometimes I let my brother
ride my bike.

ride

He rides.
Then I ride.

Then he rides.
Then I ride.

Sometimes my friends
come over to play.

"Can I play, too?"
my brother asks.

Sometimes I say,
"Okay!"

say

But sometimes I want to be
alone with my friends.

I say, "Go away, you brat!"

Then my brother gets mad.
And he won't share.

And he says,
"Go away, you brat!"

Sometimes we both share.

And that's nice.

THE END